The Poop Book

By Gramma Debbie

Illustrated by Dwain Esper

AuthorHouse™
1663 Liberty Drive
Bloomington, IN 47403
www.authorhouse.com
Phone: 1-800-839-8640

Published by AuthorHouse 08/07/2012

ISBN: 978-1-4772-5287-1 (sc)
978-1-4772-5286-4 (e)

Library of Congress Control Number: 2012913388

Any people depicted in stock imagery provided by Thinkstock are models,
and such images are being used for illustrative purposes only.
Certain stock imagery © Thinkstock.

This book is printed on acid-free paper.

authorHOUSE®

For Tobey and Grady

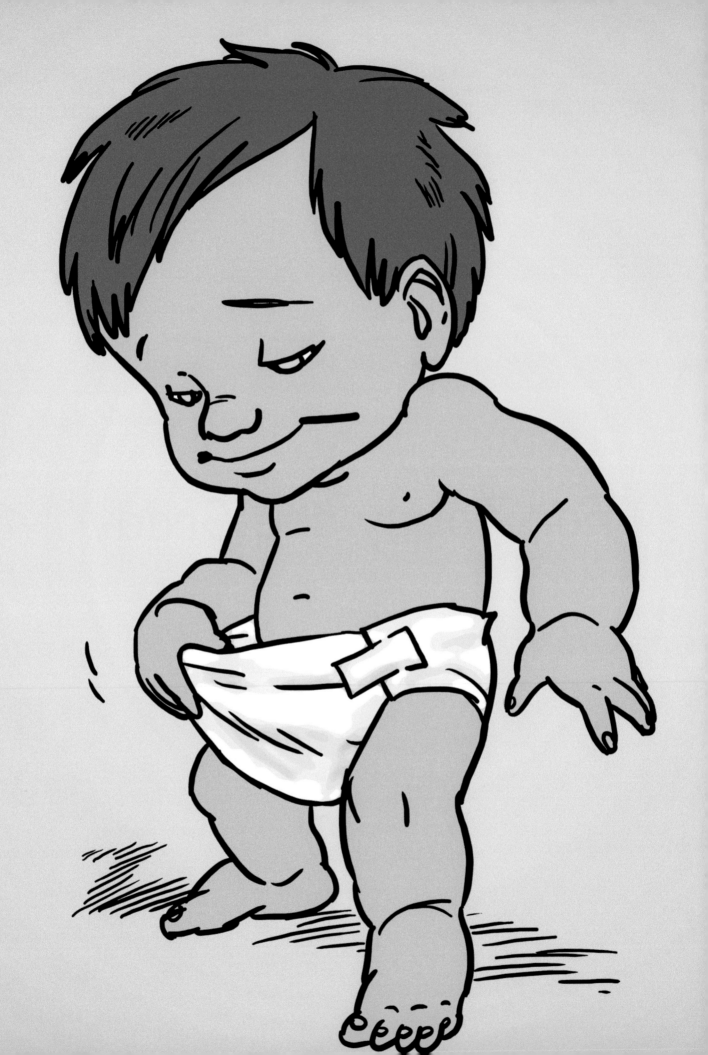

When I poop in a diaper
It makes my mom crazy

She gets mad and tells me
I'm just being lazy

Everyone says
I should poop in the potty

7

I'm a little bit scared
I'm not being naughty!

It's big and it's white
it's shiny and cold

Why can't I wait until I get old?

Mommy asks me to try
but I always say NO

Why does it matter to her where I go?

She says that it stinks and
it's sometimes like soup
That's why she cares
where I go poop

I could be like a dog
and go in the yard

19

Pick it up with a shovel
That wouldn't be hard

21

Or be like a cat
with a box to go poop
Then clean it up easy
with only one scoop

But I Know my Mom loves me
and she's always right

So I'm going to go poop
on the potty tonight

Printed in the United States
by Baker & Taylor Publisher Services